W9-BFI-574

I am big.
I can go, go, go.
You can ride in me.
What am I?

A car.
A car to ride in.

I am little.

I am red.

I am good to eat.

What am I?

An apple.

A good red apple.

I am little.

I can jump, jump, jump.

You like little me.

What am I?

A rabbit.
A rabbit that can jump.

Up and down.

Up and down.

I can go up.

I can come down.

I am fun to play with.

What am I?

A swing.

A swing that goes up and down.

I am blue.
I am up, up, up.
You have to look up
to see me.
What am I?

The sky.
The blue, blue sky.

I am not in the house.

I am out.

I am green.

I get big, big, big.

What am I?

A tree.
A big, big tree.

I run with you.
I jump with you.
I look like you.
What am I?

17

A shadow.
A shadow that looks like you.

I go up, up, up.
Away and away.
You ride in me.
What am I?

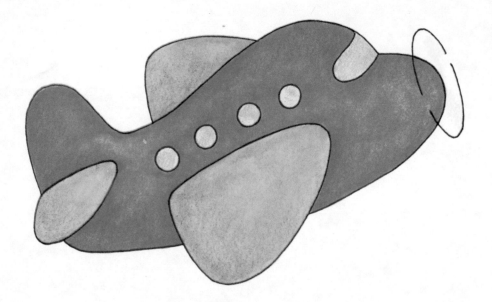

An airplane.
An airplane that goes up.

I am yellow.
I look good.
You can eat me.
What am I?

A banana.

A banana to eat.

I am big.
I can jump, jump, jump.
My baby is with me.
What am I?

A kangaroo.

A mother kangaroo with a baby.

You can go up.
You can go down.
This is fun for you
to do.
What am I?

A slide.
A slide for you to
go up and down.

I come down.
Down, down, down.
I make you run
but you like me.
What am I?

Rain.

Rain to play in.

I can not run.
I can not jump.
I am too little.
My mother helps me.
What am I?

A baby.

A little, little baby.

Margaret Hillert, author of several books in the MCP Beginning-To-Read Series, is a writer, poet, and teacher.

What Am I? uses the 66 words listed below.

a	for	like	see
airplane	fun	little	shadow
am		look(s)	sky
an	get		slide
and	go	make(s)	swing
apple	goes	me	
away	good	mother	that
	green	my	the
baby			this
banana	have	not	to
big	helps		too
blue	house	out	tree
but	how		
		play	up
can	I		
car	in	rabbit	what
come(s)	is	rain	with
	it	red	
do		ride	yellow
down	jump(s)	run	you
eat	kangaroo		